Alcazar Castle

by Grace Hansen

Abdo
FAMOUS CASTLES
Kids

Abdo Kids Jumbo is an Imprint of Abdo Kids
abdobooks.com

abdobooks.com

Published by Abdo Kids, a division of ABDO, P.O. Box 398166, Minneapolis, Minnesota 55439.
Copyright © 2022 by Abdo Consulting Group, Inc. International copyrights reserved in all countries.
No part of this book may be reproduced in any form without written permission from the publisher.
Abdo Kids Jumbo™ is a trademark and logo of Abdo Kids.

Printed in the United States of America, North Mankato, Minnesota.

052021

092021

Photo Credits: Getty Images, Granger Collection, iStock, Shutterstock,
©Wellcome Images p.17 / CC BY 4.0

Production Contributors: Teddy Borth, Jennie Forsberg, Grace Hansen
Design Contributors: Candice Keimig, Pakou Moua

Library of Congress Control Number: 2020947582
Publisher's Cataloging-in-Publication Data

Names: Hansen, Grace, author.

Title: Alcazar castle / by Grace Hansen

Description: Minneapolis, Minnesota : Abdo Kids, 2022 | Series: Famous castles | Includes online resources
   and index.

Identifiers: ISBN 9781098207274 (lib. bdg.) | ISBN 9781098208110 (ebook) | ISBN 9781098208530
   (Read-to-Me ebook)

Subjects: LCSH: Alcázar de Diego Colón (Santo Domingo, Dominican Republic)--Juvenile literature. |
   Castles--Juvenile literature. | Architecture--Juvenile literature.

Classification: DDC 728.81--dc23

Table of Contents

Alcazar of Segovia

Alcazar Castle sits high atop a cliff in beautiful Segovia, Spain. The front of the castle looks like the **bow** of a ship.

Europe

Segovia

Spain

Africa

5

Alcazar was first built on the site of a Roman fort by an Arab **dynasty**. The group wanted to show its power. The word alcazar comes from the Arabic word *al-qasr*. It means "castle" or "fortress."

Alcazar was made simply of wood at the time. Around 1100, King Alfonso VI gained control of the land.

Built in Stone

Later, King Alfonso VIII began building the stone structure seen today. Alcazar became the king and his wife's main home. Other Spanish **monarchs** would live there for years to come.

King Alfonso VIII

In 1366, a new **dynasty** began. These new rulers would build much of the newer structures. King John II built the Tower of John II of Castile. It is still the castle's highest point.

King John II

Yet another **dynasty**, beginning in 1516, would bring change to Alcazar. King Philip II added slate **spires** to the castle, but then moved his court to Madrid in 1561. The castle would serve as a prison for more than 200 years.

King Philip II

15

New Uses

In 1764, King Charles III founded the Royal Artillery School at Alcazar. Famous **chemist** Joseph Proust taught there. The school held one of the finest science labs in all of Europe.

King Charles III

Joseph Proust

In 1862, a fire badly damaged Alcazar. It wasn't until 20 years later that the castle was restored. In 1896, King Alfonso XIII ordered the castle to be given to the Ministry of War.

King Alfonso XIII

19

Today, visitors can explore the castle and museum. The grounds feature beautiful courtyards, a moat, and **lavish** rooms. The Hall of Kings can be found at the front of the castle. It holds 52 statues of former rulers.

More Facts

- There was a terrible fire at Alcazar in 1862. It greatly damaged most of the upper floors of the castle. It took 20 years for the castle to be repaired.

- The **lavish** ceiling in the Hall of Kings was **replicated** after the fire of 1862 destroyed the original.

- Islamic design style can be seen throughout the castle and its grounds. The ceilings, some of the windows, and even the gardens are all examples.

Glossary

bow – the front part of a ship or boat.

chemist – one who is an expert in the field of chemistry.

dynasty – a series of rulers from the same family or group.

lavish – being expensive or more than enough.

monarch – a ruler such as a king, queen, or emperor.

replicate – to repeat or make an exact copy of.

spire – a tall, narrow, upward structure shaped like a cone on the outside of a building.

Index

Abdo Kids
ONLINE
FREE! ONLINE MULTIMEDIA RESOURCES

Visit **abdokids.com** to access crafts, games, videos, and more!

Use Abdo Kids code
FAK7274
or scan this QR code!

New Dynamics In The Global Economy

William J. Beeman
Isaiah Frank

A Committee for Economic Development Publication

New Dynamics In The Global Economy

William J. Beeman
Isaiah Frank

with an Introductory Statement by CED Trustees

A Committee for Economic Development Publication

The Committee for Economic Development is an independent research and educational organization of two hundred business leaders and educators. CED is nonprofit, nonpartisan, and nonpolitical and is supported by contributions from business, foundations, and individuals. Its objective is to promote stable growth with rising living standards and increasing opportunities for all.

All CED policy recommendations must be approved by the Research and Policy Committee, a group of sixty trustees, which alone can speak for the organization. In issuing statements on national policy, CED often publishes background papers deemed worthy of wider circulation because of their contribution to the understanding of a public problem. This study relates to a recent CED policy statement. It has been approved for publication as supplementary paper number 248 by an editorial board of trustees and advisors. It also has been read by members of the Research Advisory Board, who have the right to submit individual memoranda of comment for publication.

While publication of this supplementary paper is authorized by CED's bylaws, its contents, except as noted above, have not been approved, disapproved, or acted upon by the Committee for Economic Development, the Board of Trustees, the Research and Policy Committee, the Research Advisory Board, the research staff, or any member or advisor of any board or committee, or any officer of CED.

Library of Congress Cataloging-in-Publication Data

Beeman, William J. (William Joseph)
   New dynamics in the global economy.

   1. International economic integration. 2. United
States--Economic policy--1981-   . 3. United States--
Commercial policy. I. Frank, Isaiah, 1917-   .
II. Title.
HF1418.5.B43 1988   337   88-25832
ISBN 0-87186-248-4 (pbk.)

First printing in bound-book form: 1988
Printed in the United States of America
Cover design: Stead Young & Rowe Inc.

PRICE: $9.50   89-3116

COMMITTEE FOR ECONOMIC DEVELOPMENT
477 Madison Avenue, New York, NY 10022 / (212) 688-2063
1700 K Street, N.W., Washington, DC 20006 / (202) 296-5860

CONTENTS

ACKNOWLEDGEMENTS

The rapid integration of global markets during the last few decades has radically changed the economic environment in which businesses and governments operate. This paper was prepared at the request of CED Trustees who are concerned about the lack of accessible information on the extent of market integration and on the implications of this development for national economic policies. However, as with other supplementary papers authorized by CED, the views expressed in this paper are the responsibility of the authors.

The authors wish to acknowledge their gratitude to CED Trustees who provided many insights on the globalization of markets, based on their vast business experience in international markets. We also received valuable suggestions for improving this paper from members of the CED Research Advisory Board. Special thanks are also extended to the CED staff, Seong Park and Kate Jones, who assisted Mr. Beeman in researching several of the regulatory issues and to Janet Dewar who assisted Professor Frank. We also wish to thank Barbara Willard, Valerie de la Cruz, and Mary Hiatt for their assistance in the preparation of this paper.

We also gratefully acknowledge the John M. Olin Foundation, Inc. for their generous support of CED's globalization project. This paper is a part of that project.

Bill Beeman
Vice President and Director of Macroeconomic Studies
Committee for Economic Development

Isaiah Frank
William L. Clayton Professor of International Economics
The Johns Hopkins University

INTRODUCTORY STATEMENT

by the Undersigned CED Trustees

The decline in the economic significance of national boundaries and the increasing globalization of markets are fundamentally changing the way we in the United States need to carry out business both at home and abroad.

As trustees of the Committee for Economic Development (CED), we are convinced that unless we adopt economic policies based on a broad understanding of what globalization actually means for this country, we may never achieve the competitive position we need to assure a strong economy in the future and continued real growth in the standard of living of U.S. citizens.

Many companies, after considerable and often painful adjustments, have come to recognize the nature of the global forces that are shaping their markets. These firms have adopted basic changes in their corporate strategies that permit them to operate effectively in an environment of increasing international integration of finance, technology, production, and even human resources. Where trade-sensitive firms have been slow to respond to the new economic reality, they have either failed or suffered serious damage from loss of competitiveness.

The American people, on the other hand, while perceiving that things are not what they were, often view the globalization phenomenon narrowly in terms of either the foreign goods they consume (e.g., cars, electronics, clothing, toys) or the jobs they see being lost in our hardest-hit industries.

Many government policy makers, often influenced by public perceptions, also do not grasp the pervasive dynamics of global markets. They see global integration as a threat to economic growth in this country but not as a source of opportunity. As a result, they do not recognize the need to reform outmoded policies that were developed in an era when most Americans felt they had little stake in foreign economic developments, and they continue to adopt policies that are not appropriate for a global economy. Even in the early 1980s, the United States pursued excessively expansive fiscal policies at the same time that our major foreign competitors adopted restrictive fiscal policies, and little thought was given to the serious negative effects this combination would have on U.S. international competitiveness.

This single-mindedness continues to manifest itself. For example, the 1986 Tax Reform Act was enacted with comparatively little attention paid to its possible effects on the ability of U.S. companies to compete internationally.

Even in areas where international implications generally receive more careful consideration, such as trade policy, policy makers often attempt to establish barriers to globalization rather than help the nation benefit from the opportunities afforded by greater economic integration.

To help convey an understanding of the new reality, we commissioned New Dynamics in the Global Economy, a concise overview of the globalization process and its public policy implications. The paper identifies the primary global forces that now significantly shape the U.S. economy and intensify particular major challenges facing U.S. policy makers, such as the serious problems of worker adjustment, poor-quality education, and the inadequacy of domestic saving to finance domestic investment. At the same time, it points out where integration of global markets offers opportunities for large gains through economies of scale, more widely available technology, and a more rational allocation of resources within and among countries. The paper indicates those areas of current macroeconomic, regulatory, and other policies that clearly need reform; it also points out those areas where our understanding is weak and additional research is vitally needed.

CED plans to launch a number of studies on these and other policy issues affected by globalization. We hope that other organizations and citizens interested in public policy will do the same. In anticipation of likely consideration of new revenue-raising measures next year, we believe that high-priority attention must be given to the impact of tax policy on international competitiveness. Trade and macroeconomic policies also deserve high priority, as does the international regulatory climate.

Careful analysis of these issues by all concerned is a prerequisite to effective national policy making in a global economy. We hope that this paper will contribute to that analysis.

ix

Chapter 1

INTRODUCTION

The world economy and the place of the United States in it are fundamentally different today from what they were twenty-five years ago. This change is not the result of any single event nor of any sudden shift in the direction of economic activity. Rather, it is the cumulative effect of trends that have been under way for decades and that in recent years have reached dimensions suggesting differences in kind, not just in degree.

Various phrases have been used more or less interchangeably to describe these trends: the "globalization of markets;" the "increasing integration of the world economy;" and "growing international economic interdependence." Whatever words are used, the essence of what has been going on is a steady decline in the economic significance of national political boundaries. Today, the economic links and interactions among countries have become so close that the distinction between domestic and foreign transactions has all but disappeared.

Broadly speaking, two developments underlie the increasing integration of the world economy. One is technological: the explosive advances in the speed and effectiveness of international communication and transportation and the concomitant shrinkage in their real costs. The other is economic: the reduction or dismantlement of national barriers to the international movement of goods, services, technology, and capital. A dramatic example of the combined effect of these developments was the virtually simultaneous collapse of the securities markets in the world's principal financial centers on October 19, 1987 (Black Monday).

Despite the forces of globalization, nation-states retain distinctive characteristics that condition their reactions to increasing economic interdependence. History and culture, values and goals, government and business institutions, and systems of public and private decision making all affect the extent to which individual nations accept or resist further integration into the world economy. The evidence suggests that although business has for the most part adapted to globalization, governments have frequently intervened to counteract this process or control its consequences.

Although the phenomenon of increasing interdependence is yet to be fully assimilated in our thinking, the globalization of markets, production, technology, and finance has profound economic effects and implications for policy. On the one hand, the increased size of markets and the free movement of resources present opportunities for large gains through economies of scale, wider competition, and a more rational allocation of resources within and among countries. Yet, at the same time, more open economic borders pose major competitive challenges for domestic industry, create serious problems of worker adjustment, and call into question the adequacy of our defense industrial base. Increasing interdependence also tends to undermine the effectiveness of national economic policies at both the macroeconomic and the microeconomic level.

Recent experience has shown, for example, that in a large open economy such as the United States, international capital mobility and flexible exchange rates have altered the way in which fiscal and monetary policy work. In the early 1980s, expansionary fiscal and tight monetary policies (not offset by increases in private saving) reinforced each other in appreciating the dollar and worsening the trade imbalance. The massive trade deficit has been eroding this country's capacity for leadership and is inducing a more inward thrust in U.S. trade policy, as demonstrated by the espousal of a new and narrow concept of reciprocity.

Regulatory and tax policies have also been affected by the increase in economic interdependence. Most such policies were designed in an era when economic developments abroad had a relatively small effect on our domestic economy and when most American corporations had little stake in foreign activity. When laws and regulations were adopted, their impact on international competitiveness was often not taken into consideration. Today, as global influences on our economy become pervasive, many public policies need to be restructured to reflect the reality of global markets.

Two types of effects on regulation and taxation stem from world economic integration. On the one hand, integration reduces the effectiveness and complicates the administration of domestic tax and regulatory policies by giving domestic firms a choice of national jurisdiction to which to subject their affairs. On the other hand, integration helps to limit excessive government intervention in the private sector. Most governments are concerned with the conflict between their desire to maintain the effectiveness of national regulation and taxation and their desire to avoid policies that put domestic firms at a competitive disadvantage because of lower taxes and regulatory standards in other countries.

This paper describes the trends toward globalization and considers their impact on macroeconomic and microeconomic policy making. Fiscal policy, including the tax structure and its effects on national saving and investment, is considered, along with the international spillover effects of domestic monetary policy. In the microeconomic field, we discuss trade policy as well as a variety of business regulations that have cross-border effects. Consideration is also given to some of the implications of the decline in U.S. economic supremacy. We also briefly explore the general strategies available to help resolve the public policy dilemmas posed by closer international economic integration in a world politically divided among nation-states.

Chapter 2

TRENDS IN INTERNATIONAL INTEGRATION

Globalization of Markets for Goods and Services

World trade has grown far more rapidly than world production, implying a closer integration of the global economy. The disparate trends are particularly striking for the manufacturing sector (see Table 1, below). For the industrial countries as a whole, the consequence is that merchandise trade (exports and imports) rose from only 12.7 percent of gross national product (GNP) in 1960 to almost 30 percent by 1984.[1] For the United States, the ratio of trade in goods and services to GNP increased from 10.1 percent in 1960 to 21.6 percent in 1984.

Table 1

Growth of World Merchandise Trade and Production
(average annual percentage change in volume)

	1960-1969	1970-1979	1980-1983	1984	1985
All merchandise					
Exports	8.5	5.5	0.5	9.5	3.0
Production	6.0	4.0	0.0	5.5	3.0
Manufacturing					
Exports	10.5	7.5	2.0	12.0	6.0
Production	7.4	0.5	1.0	7.0	4.0

Source: General Agreement on Tariffs and Trade, International Trade 1985-86 (Geneva: GATT, 1986) p. 13.

The increase in world trade reflects the same phenomena that underlie economic integration in general: reductions in government barriers to trade and rapid technological developments that have greatly diminished the costs of international transport and communications. The average tariff level of the industrial countries has been reduced from

---

[1] The tendency of world trade to grow faster than output extends back to 1800. The only exception was the period from 1913 to the 1950s, when the long-term trend was interrupted by wars, the Great Depression, and increases in trade barriers. Simon Kuznets, "Quantitative Aspects of the Growth of Nations: Level and Structure of Foreign Trade," *Economic Development and Cultural Change* 15, no. 2, Part II (January 1967): p. 5.

about 40 percent in the mid-1930s to about 6 percent now. In real terms, the cost of an international telephone message is today only 5 percent of what it was thirty-five years ago. Fares for international air travel have also come down sharply, costing today, in real terms, only about 10 percent of fares in the late 1930s.[2]

In addition to the greater openness of the world economy, international trade in manufactured products has been boosted by the tendency toward convergence in the per capita incomes and demand patterns of the industrial countries. Countries with similar patterns of demand have tended to have higher volumes of trade with each other. Moreover, where tastes overlap, a high proportion of a country's foreign trade in manufactures tends to be intraindustry trade (i.e., the export and import of differentiated products falling within the same industrial category.)[3]

As a result of these trends, there is scarcely a market in the industrial countries today that is untouched by developments in other countries. Even producers who are inclined to think in domestic terms and who are not concerned with foreign market opportunities quickly come to realize that their counterparts abroad are thinking globally. Consequently, the competition they face at home is from foreign as well as domestic firms. Today, few in business (including farmers) can afford to be unconcerned with such things as exchange rates and the state of the world economy. Government policies abroad as well as at home inevitably affect competitiveness and profitability.

Another fundamental change in the structure of world markets is the emergence of rapidly growing economies in the Third World. Before the debt crisis erupted in 1982, U.S. trade with the developing world exceeded 40 percent of its total trade. Whereas markets in the developed countries are maturing, the potential for rapid growth in trade with the newly industrialized countries is very great. This is widely recognized in the case of the East Asian countries but less so now in the case of the Latin American nations. However, the current debt crisis does not diminish the long-term potential for growth in this sizable market.

Higher standards of living and more rapid economic growth are among the benefits of expanding trade under an open global system.

[2] Richard Cooper, "The United States as an Open Economy," in *How Open Is the U.S. Economy?* ed. R. W. Hafer (Lexington, MA: Lexington Books, 1986), pp. 10-13.

[3] David Greenaway and Chris Milner, "The Growth and Significance of Intra-Industry Trade," in *Changes in the Structure of World Trade*, ed. J. Black and A. MacBean (London: Macmillan, 1988), Chapter 4. The growth of intraindustry trade has also occurred in North-South trade because of the tendency of the North to specialize in high-quality and the South in low-quality products within the same industrial category. See Harry Flam and Elhanan Helpman, "Vertical Product Differentiation and North-South Trade," *American Economic Review* 77, no. 5 (December 1987): p. 821.

These results come not only from the static gains brought about by the more efficient use of a country's existing resources in response to the pressures of international competition: at least as important are the dynamic gains from the stimulus to investment, learning, and entrepreneurship that comes with expanding markets and exposure to new products, technologies, ideas, and standards.

At the same time, however, the more open global trading system has exposed U.S. industries to severe competitive pressures. As a result of rapid industrialization in many developing countries, the comparative advantage in some industries has shifted away from the United States. This natural economic movement was accentuated in the first half of the decade by the overvaluation of the U.S. dollar, which damaged the international competitive position of U.S. industries across the board. The combined effect of these conditions has been the complete withdrawal from the market of some firms that might have remained competitive with the more realistic exchange rates that now prevail.

The postwar trend toward the liberalization of international trade can no longer be taken for granted. Although tariffs have continued to come down, nontariff barriers have proliferated in recent years. A recent World Bank study shows that 27 percent of all imports of the industrial countries and more than 34 percent of their imports from developing countries are affected by nontariff barriers.[4] Such measures have a protective effect far more serious than that of tariffs and are extremely costly to the domestic economy. For example, current quotas on textile and apparel imports cost American consumers $20 billion a year, or $100,000 per job saved in the textile and apparel industries.[5] How to stem the drift toward protectionism is one of today's major public policy issues.

Another issue is how to adapt the system to new developments such as the expanding role of trade in services and the increasing importance of more effective international protection of intellectual property rights.

Internationalization of Production

Companies manufacturing a particular product increasingly think of the advantages of alternative international locations rather than purely in terms of domestic production. The globalization of production has two principal dimensions. One is direct investment in a foreign affiliate, frequently in conjunction with local partners. Much of this type of investment has been induced by the need to leapfrog actual or expected import restrictions in order to sell in a large or rapidly growing local

---

[4] J. J. Nogues, A. Olechowski, and L. A. Winters, "The Extent of Nontariff Barriers to Industrial Countries' Imports," *The World Bank Economic Review* 1, no. 1 (September 1986): pp. 192, 194.

[5] William R. Cline, *The Future of World Trade in Textiles and Apparel* (Washington, D.C.: Institute for International Economics, 1987), p. 15.

market (e.g., IBM in Mexico, Honda in the United States). Increasingly, however, it is motivated by cost considerations favoring the establishment of an export base abroad for the purpose of selling products both to the home market and to third-country markets (e.g., Xerox in the Far East). In addition, firms in sectors such as banking and consumer products establish affiliates abroad in order to service local markets more effectively.

The second dimension of the internationalization of production is the growing trend toward sourcing abroad for individual processes and components within a chain of production. For example, U.S. auto companies purchase engines from Brazil, and U.S. companies assemble electronic components in plants located across the border in Mexico. The intermediate components and foreign processing may come from affiliates of the parent company, as is common in electronics. But in other industries (e.g., apparel), they are often imported from completely independent firms, thus differentiating the relationship from the traditional private direct investment model of the internationalization of production. The ultimate stage in this process is reached when firms import final products from foreign competitors and attach their own nameplates to them (e.g., the Dodge Colt is made by Mitsubishi). In the automotive and electronic sectors particularly, the nationality of a product is becoming increasingly elusive. The trend toward foreign sourcing has been accentuated in recent years by sharp exchange rate fluctuations.

The two dimensions of the globalization of production are reflected in the major role multinational companies play in world trade. According to Raymond Vernon, as much as half of the world exports of nonagricultural products originates in companies that are units in a multinational network, and perhaps a quarter of world nonagricultural trade consists of exchanges between units of individual multinational firms.[6] In short, international trade and investment are intimately linked.

Given the role of multinationals in international trade, it is not surprising that the companies in the best position to respond to rapid change have been those which have achieved a thorough integration of their worldwide research and development, production, purchasing, and marketing activities. This integration, usually facilitated by highly sophisticated management information systems, permits the international flexibility required to cope with significant changes in competitive conditions such as those induced by currency valuation swings. For some companies, however, total integration may not be appropriate. For example, the international food processing and personal products industries may conduct research on a global scale, but they adapt their production to locally available supplies and unique demand conditions.

Although the globalization process is bringing substantial benefits to all participating countries, it is severely accentuating problems of domestic worker adjustment in individual U.S. industries. The industries most

---

[6] Raymond Vernon, "Global Interdependence in a Historic Perspective," in *Interdependence and Cooperation in Tomorrow's World* (Paris: OECD, 1987), p. 14.

acutely affected by the new competitive challenges may choose to move some operations abroad, but workers, by and large, do not have that option. This situation underlines the importance of measures to increase the flexibility of the U.S. labor force to respond to domestic changes induced by international conditions. Among the actions needed are educational reforms for a changing market, job-training programs, and relocation assistance. Improvements in the portability of health benefits and pension rights would also increase the readiness of workers to move to other jobs. At the same time, organized labor and management must share the responsibility for improving the productivity and competitiveness of U.S. industry.

Multinational companies are likely to continue to employ local citizens in the countries where they operate (whether they are foreign companies hiring American workers in the United States or U.S. companies hiring foreigners abroad). However, they are likely to encounter an increasing need for scarce, but internationally astute talent at the management level.

Another consequence of the internationalization of production is that units of a multinational enterprise operating in different jurisdictions are often subject to conflicting national government policies. This problem is perhaps most familiar in the case of security export controls, but it has also arisen in the fields of antitrust, corporate disclosure, and transfer pricing. Generally, the problems have been resolved through quiet diplomacy or the efforts of corporations to present the facts of their cases to governments. Occasionally, however, they have escalated into major international disputes (e.g., the Soviet gas pipeline case) that have detracted from our ability to deal with larger issues.

Between 1979 and 1986, the stock of foreign direct investment in the United States increased by 280 percent (from $55 billion to $209 billion), compared with a growth of only 38 percent (from $188 billion to $260 billion) in U.S. direct investment abroad.[7] Although the stock of U.S. direct investment abroad still exceeds that of foreign investment in this country, the large capital inflows in recent years have given rise to fears of the "buying up" of America by foreigners.

Net inflows of capital from abroad are, of course, simply the counterpart of the U.S. deficit in its current account. Therefore, they can be reduced only by a narrowing of the trade deficit. From the standpoint of limiting volatility in financial markets, it is better to have the deficit financed by direct investment, implying a long-term commitment to the U.S. economy, than through the acquisition by foreigners of liquid U.S. financial assets. Moreover, the direct participation in American business by internationally oriented European and Japanese companies may improve U.S. export performance by opening up new marketing opportunities abroad for products manufactured in America. New restrictions on private foreign direct investment should therefore be avoided.

---

[7] *Economic Report of the President* (Washington, D.C.: U.S. Government Printing Office, February 1988), Table B-106.

Recently, there has been some direct investment by foreign governments and state enterprises (e.g., the purchase by the Kuwait Petroleum Company of a sizable interest in British Petroleum Company). This type of investment bears close watching to ensure that it does not involve direct or indirect subsidization by foreign governments that would provide a competitive advantage over domestic firms.

Internationalization of Technology

The pace of technological innovation is a driving force in the world economy.

The world's body of scientific knowledge probably doubles every decade. The United States, with about 5 percent of the world's population, generates almost half of the world's scientific information. This is down from nearly 75 percent a decade ago and, in another decade, it may drop further to only a third of the total. This decrease is not because the United States will be generating less, but because the other 95 percent of the world will be generating more. This torrent produces new technology so fast that most technology becomes obsolete within 5-7 years. In electronics, it's 2-3 years.[8]

There are three ways in which this outpouring of new technology is being internationalized: the international transfer of technology, both by transnational licensing and through the operations of multinational enterprises; the cross-border education of students in science and engineering; and joint research and development by individuals and companies of different nationalities.

Much of modern technology has no distinctive nationality, in the sense that it is developed in institutions that draw talented specialists from countries around the world. The scientists and engineers who work in American universities and research laboratories, many of them foreign nationals, regard themselves as members of a global community of researchers who work on joint projects, meet periodically in international conferences, exchange articles, and publish their results worldwide. Moreover, American companies are setting up research laboratories abroad and staffing them with foreign engineers and scientists. Examples include the Du Pont and IBM laboratories in Japan and IBM's Zurich laboratory, where a German and a Swiss physicist jointly discovered the new class of ceramic superconductor material. Similarly, foreign companies are acquiring or setting up high-technology firms and laboratories in the United States (e.g., Ciba-Geigy's acquisition of Spectra-Physics, the world's largest maker and developer of lasers). Joint ventures for the manufacture of high-technology products are also increasing (e.g., AT&T's joint venture with a Korean firm, Goldstar Semiconductor, to manufacture public telephone exchanges and local area networks). In sum, what Robert

---

[8] William Van Dusen Wishard, "Perspective '87" (Washington, D.C.: U.S. Department of Commerce), p. 16.

Reich calls <u>techno-globalism</u> has become a common American organizing principle for developing new technologies.[9]

As industrial technology has developed, it has increasingly become an internationally marketable commodity. The transfer process occurs both within the operations of multinational enterprises and through their contractual arrangements to provide technology and services to unaffiliated companies. Receipts from the export of technology from firms based in five developed countries (United States, Great Britain, France, West Germany, and Japan) have increased considerably, from less than $2 billion in 1965 to around $11 billion in 1983.[10]

The close relationship between international flows of investment and of technology is reflected in the high share of technology receipts from affiliated firms out of total receipts for technological services. In the case of American companies, for example, 78 percent of foreign receipts from technology in 1983 was from affiliated companies.

The transfer of knowledge rather than financial capital should be regarded as the essence of foreign direct investment because multinational enterprises typically raise substantial proportions of capital in the countries in which they operate. In a number of developing countries, the prime consideration in permitting a foreign firm to establish an affiliate is its technological rather than its financial contribution.

A major challenge for American industry is to improve its performance in converting research and invention into marketable products. Case after case of American technological breakthroughs followed by Japanese domination of the commercial applications exist. Perhaps the most noteworthy example is the videocassette recorder (VCR), which is an American invention conceived in the 1960s by Ampex and RCA. Today, not one American company makes VCRs. All 13 million units sold in the United States in 1986 were made in Japan or Korea.

Part of the problem may be the asymmetry in the extent to which U.S. and foreign engineers keep up with technological developments in other countries. A recent report of the National Academy of Engineering notes that fewer than 1,000 Americans are studying technical subjects such as engineering, computer science, physics, and business management in foreign universities. In contrast, there are almost 200,000 foreign students studying technical subjects in American universities. This discrepancy may be partly due to the superiority of advanced scientific and technical

[9] Robert B. Reich, "The Rise of Techno-Nationalism," *The Atlantic Monthly* (May 1987): p. 64. The exceptions to techno-globalism are the restrictions on the participation of the Soviet Union and its allies in joint research and on the transfer of sensitive technologies to those countries.

[10] Katherine Marton, "Technology Transfer to Developing Countries via Multinationals," *The World Economy* (December 1986).

education in the United States. However, there is also a language factor. Although most Japanese engineers read English well enough to understand technical journals published in the United States, there are probably no more than a few dozen American engineers capable of reading technical Japanese.[11] An element of parochialism may also be present in American attitudes toward Japanese scientific and technical information as reflected in the low demand for English translations offered by United States federal agencies and private companies.[12]

The global market provides an opportunity for companies to reduce the high cost of research and development through economies of scale. Moreover, the short life cycle characteristic of many new technologies in the markets of the industrial countries provides an incentive to seek markets in the developing countries, where the cycle can usually be extended.

The globalization of the market for technology has underlined the importance of worldwide legal protection for invention and innovation. Whether U.S. patent law is an appropriate model in all cases may be an open question, but the absence of adequate protection in many countries is a major obstacle to the international transfer of technology. For example, U.S. agrichemical companies have not introduced proprietary products into the Indian market until the expiration of their patent life because of fear of piracy.

A complex of international agreements exists for the protection of intellectual property rights (patents, copyrights, trademarks). Generally, they rely on national treatment as the basis for international protection. However, because of the inadequacy of domestic legislation in many countries (especially in the Third World), national treatment provides an insufficient guarantee. Moreover, existing agreements provide neither enforcement powers nor means for the settlement of disputes. The United States has proposed making the General Agreement on Tariffs and Trade (GATT) the focal point for achieving adequate standards, enforcing such standards, and settling disputes.

Finally, there is the problem of how best to protect the most important new technologies, especially computer software, semiconductor chips, and advances in biotechnology. Because some of the new technologies do not fit unambiguously into any of the existing categories of intellectual property, their eligibility for legal protection is uncertain in many countries, and piracy is widespread.

---

[11] Report of the National Academy of Engineering, *Washington Post*, August 20, 1987.

[12] "Japanese Scientific and Technological Literature Information: The Demand in the U.S. Remains Low," *Science* 238 (November 1987): p. 1032.

Integration of World Financial Markets

The globalization of markets has a financial as well as a real dimension. The pool of savings today is worldwide, and intermediaries that mobilize those savings for use by investors know no national boundaries. This phenomenon is partly a reflection of the rapid growth of Eurocurrency markets that are unhampered by any national regulation and the trend toward mobilizing savings through larger institutions (not only banks but also pension funds, insurance companies, mutual funds, and other entities) that have the sophistication and interest to access markets worldwide through a variety of instruments. The entire process has been facilitated by the progressive deregulation and liberalization of national capital markets, the trend toward the securitization of loans,[13] and of course, rapid technological progress in computers and telecommunications.

One indicator of the increase in financial interdependence is the growth of international bank credit as reported by the Bank for International Settlements (BIS). After netting out most interbank claims, the BIS series shows an increase from $12 billion in 1964 to $1,485 billion in 1985, a rate of growth amounting to 25.8 percent compounded annually. This contrasts with a growth rate for the nominal value of international trade in goods and services of only 12.4 percent over the same period.[14]

The high degree of volatility of exchange rates in recent years has been accompanied by institutional changes facilitating hedging against currency conversion risks. This development and persistent misalignment of exchange rates has accelerated the trend toward globalization. Under the Bretton Woods system, exchange rate considerations were less compelling in inducing money managers to consider investments in currencies other than their own except during those discrete intervals when adjustments in the pegged rate seemed imminent. Today, simple prudence dictates that major borrowers and lenders continuously take likely changes in exchange rates into account and consider opportunities available in other currencies. Transactions in foreign exchange currently amount to over $200 billion a day.[15]

Another important phenomenon underlying the internationalization of finance has been the massive payment imbalances of the 1970s and 1980s. The surpluses amassed by the members of the Organization of Petroleum Exporting Countries (OPEC) in the 1970s and by the Japanese and West

---

[13] Securitization has two aspects: the increasing tendency of big borrowers to sell their securities directly to investors and the tendency of the banks themselves to convert their loans into marketable securities. The resulting enhancement of the liquidity of debt obligations facilitates the globalization of credit markets.

[14] Ralph Bryant, *International Financial Intermediation* (Washington, D.C.: The Brookings Institution, 1987), Table 3.1, p. 22.

[15] John G. Heimann, Speech to the Forum de l'Expansion, Paris, May 19, 1987.

Germans in the 1980s have constituted the main sources of savings to finance the excess expenditure of the developing countries in the first case ("recycling") and of the United States in the second. In both cases, the national imbalances between domestic production and expenditure have been enormous and have required international financial intermediation on an unprecedented scale to close the gap.

In the absence of an inward flow of capital to finance excess U.S. expenditure, interest rates would have been driven higher, and business investment as well as interest-sensitive consumer expenditures (e.g., on homes and automobiles) would have been crowded out. Our international accounts would have been forced into balance, but at the cost of reduced consumption and private investment in the United States.

However, the benefits of international financial intermediation are not limited to facilitating the transfer of funds from nations that are excess savers to those that are excess spenders. Even if all countries were in balance internally and externally, so that net international capital flows were zero for each country, substantial benefits would be garnered through the increase in gross cross-border financial transactions. Such transactions permit a more efficient allocation of world resources than would otherwise occur by providing enhanced opportunities for savers and investors to diversify their assets and liabilities with respect to such characteristics as risk, maturity, currency, and debt-to-equity convertibility. These benefits are analogous to the gains from trade that widen world consumption possibilities. As with trade in goods, some countries enjoy a comparative advantage in the provision of financial services because of factors such as economies of scale and international differences in liquidity preferences.

The major issue in international finance is how to maximize the net benefits of global integration of capital markets. Whereas the impediments to international trade in goods consist largely of border measures such as tariffs and import quotas, the constraints on international financial integration are mainly internal. They arise from the complexity and diversity of national financial infrastructures that form the basis of the global financial system. In most countries, these infrastructures, which include domestic systems of regulation and supervision, accounting, taxation, and clearing, are inadequately geared to global markets.

Chapter 3

MACROECONOMIC EFFECTS OF GLOBALIZATION

The combination of the greater openness of the U.S. economy, a high degree of international capital mobility, and flexible exchange rates has altered the effects of macroeconomic policies on the domestic economy.[16]

Fiscal and Monetary Policy

On the fiscal side, measures intended to stimulate the U.S. economy through tax reductions or expenditure increases have a diluted effect in increasing aggregate demand for U.S. goods. Because of the higher marginal propensity to import in a more open economy, a greater part of the stimulus to private economic activity leaks abroad.

This attenuation of the effects of fiscal expansion as the economy becomes more open is augmented under a regime of flexible exchange rates. Assuming no change in monetary policy, expansionary fiscal measures raise interest rates and attract foreign capital.[17] The capital inflow leads to an appreciation of the currency, which in turn adversely affects the trade balance. Again, the stimulative effect of the initial expansionary action is weakened. However, the weakening is offset to some extent by the contribution that the capital inflow makes in limiting the rise of interest rates.

Whereas the impact of fiscal policy is attenuated in an open economy with flexible rates, the conventional effects of monetary policy are augmented. Monetary policy has traditionally operated through its effects on interest rates and the prices of financial assets. Easier money leads initially to lower interest rates that encourage expenditures on interest-sensitive goods, especially housing and capital goods. It also stimulates spending by increasing the wealth in private hands as a consequence of the rise in the prices of financial assets. Under flexible exchange rates, however, a further expansionary impulse is transmitted through the effect of lower interest rates in depreciating the currency and inducing an improvement in the trade balance. Opposite effects, including a weakening of the trade balance are induced by tighter monetary policy.

---

[16] Cooper, "The United States as an Open Economy."

[17] Care should be taken to avoid generalizing the effect of fiscal expansion in attracting foreign capital. Extreme examples of the opposite effect are the capital flight associated with highly expansionary fiscal policy and accommodative monetary policy in a number of Latin American countries in the early 1980s.

In the early 1980s, the United States pursued expansionary fiscal and tight monetary policies that, in the absence of offsetting increases in private savings, reinforced each other in causing the dollar to appreciate. At the same time, our principal overseas trading partners relied on the opposite combination (tight fiscal and easy monetary policies), which exerted downward pressure on the exchange values of their currencies. This mismatch led to a rapid worsening in the U.S. trade deficit and steeply rising surpluses in Germany and Japan.

In the public mind, the soaring U.S. trade deficit has been widely attributed to a deterioration in the real determinants of competitiveness rather than to monetary factors. Lags in U.S. productivity growth, flaws in U.S. management and labor, and "unfair" trade practices of other countries have been cited. Whatever validity exists in these explanations, they have in fact been overshadowed quantitatively by the effects of macroeconomic policies in the United States and abroad.

The dangers of mismatched policies are magnified when the domestic effects of foreign macroeconomic policies are unwelcome. In that case, a country may be forced to take unwanted action to counter the policies of foreign countries. Some governments have attempted to offset the depressing effects on their net exports of an expansionary monetary policy abroad with an expansive monetary policy of their own. There is a risk that such behavior will lead to a sequential easing of monetary policy to reduce the value of currencies in order to remain competitive. Although such expansionary policies may temporarily raise incomes, they are likely to lead to extreme inflationary pressures. In principle, the same income levels could be achieved without such inflation if competitive devaluations were avoided through greater coordination of policies.

On the other hand, one country may be able to exploit the policies of other countries to its own benefit. For example, one country may rely on the so-called locomotive effect of another's expansionary fiscal policy to achieve its objectives for growth in output without incurring the cost of an expansionary policy of its own. In extreme cases, such a mismatch may lead to a dangerous imbalance in trade, huge foreign debts, and economic instability.

Coordination of Macroeconomic Policies

The remedy commonly proposed for the disequilibrium resulting from the mismatch of national macroeconomic policies is international coordination. Coordination does not mean that different countries' national goals are identical. Rather, it implies a mutual willingness to adjust behavior at the margin in a way that advances the interests of all participants. To accomplish coordination in this sense requires a common understanding of the linkages among national economies and the political will and ability to make the necessary domestic policy adjustments.

In principle, the coordination of macroeconomic policies can improve the outcome for all countries involved. For example, when a country expands its fiscal policy, it tends to shift its current-account balance with other countries toward deficit. If all countries expand at the same time, however, increased growth could be achieved without a deterioration in the current account. The potential and the incentive for such economic policy coordination has increased as the world economy has become more integrated.[18]

Nevertheless, attempts to coordinate domestic and foreign macroeconomic policies have been at best only partially successful. The benefits may be too small and the differences in policy goals too large for systematic macroeconomic policy coordination.[19] Differences in financial structure and the evolution of financial institutions may complicate attempts to coordinate policies. There have also been disagreements about how economic policies affect national economies. Finally, some nations have chosen to pursue a mercantilist policy of protection of home markets and subsidization of exports without regard to the damage to the global economy that would result if all countries were to act as though they could be surplus countries. Such policies create tension, distrust, and an atmosphere that is certainly not conducive to successful negotiation of coordinated policies.

Despite these obstacles, efforts to achieve some degree of economic policy coordination have long been a part of relations between the United States and other advanced industrial countries. For nearly three decades following the Bretton Woods conference, exchange rates were fixed, and the interaction of macroeconomic policies was guided by the attempt of monetary authorities to maintain a fixed relationship between foreign currencies and the U.S. dollar. After the introduction of floating exchange rates in 1973, monetary authorities hoped to focus more on domestic objectives. But the resulting instability in exchange rates and stronger-than-anticipated interaction of policy effects led to frequent demands for macroeconomic policy coordination.

The economic turbulence of the 1970s and the 1980s resulted in more frequent meetings devoted to the coordination of national macroeconomic policies. Negotiations after the 1973 oil price shock were credited with reducing pressures for import restrictions but were unable to keep most major countries from switching to more restrictive policies that contributed to a worldwide recession.[20] The 1978 Bonn Summit, in which Japan and West Germany agreed to fiscal expansion in return for deregulation of U.S. oil prices, is often cited as a successful example of coordination. However, many now regard the outcome as undesirable in light of the ensuing inflation.

---

[18] Stanley Fischer, *International Macroeconomic Policy Coordination*, National Bureau of Economic Research Working Paper No. 2244 (May 1987): pp. 1-2.

[19] Fischer, *International Macroeconomic Policy Coordination*, p. 49.

[20] George A. Kahn, "International Policy Coordination in an Interdependent World," Federal Reserve Bank of Kansas City, *Economic Review* (March 1987): p. 15.

The second oil price shock in 1979, was followed by the adoption of deflationary monetary policies in many countries that resulted in a worldwide recession in the early 1980s. Proposals for a coordinated stimulative policy to encourage recovery from the recession were not widely supported. Meanwhile, a huge appreciation of the dollar occurred between 1981 and 1985 largely in response to the restrictive U.S. monetary policy of the early 1980s and the stimulative fiscal policy thereafter. The rise in the dollar was the primary reason for the shift in the U.S. trade position from a surplus in 1981 to a huge deficit in 1986.

Between 1981 and 1985, the U.S. government argued against intervention in currency markets, contending that the strong dollar reflected foreign investors' approval of U.S. economic policies.[21] At the September 1985 Plaza meeting of the Group of Five (G-5) countries (United States, the United Kingdom, West Germany, Japan, and France), the United States changed its position and acknowledged that the high dollar was a problem for American industry. The United States and other countries then joined together in an exchange market intervention designed to reduce the relative value of the dollar, which had already been declining for several months.

In early 1987, after the dollar had declined more sharply than expected, the United States and other countries met at the Louvre and adopted a program that called for intervention to achieve exchange rate stability. However, this policy, reaffirmed in June 1987 in Venice and in September 1987 at the International Monetary Fund-World Bank meetings, did not prove successful in stemming the dollar's decline.

Following this experience, the prevailing view seems to be that sterilized market intervention cannot achieve the desired exchange rate objective unless there is a corresponding change in underlying fiscal policies.[22] Currently, there are strong demands here and abroad for a sharp reduction in the U.S. budget deficit and a more expansionary fiscal policy abroad, particularly in Germany and Japan, where very large trade surpluses persist.

However, coordination alone cannot solve the mismatch problem. Inevitably, even those governments most cognizant of their interdependence and willing to coordinate to a significant extent will follow economic policies that reflect their own circumstances and interests. The United States, for example, cannot rely mainly on Germany and Japan to adopt expansionary policies to help it solve domestic economic problems. However, if this country adopts policies that effectively reduce its budget and trade deficits, the impact on the domestic economies of countries in balance-of-payments surplus will induce expansionary policies that no amount of exhortation could accomplish. Coordination may be desirable in

---

[21] Martin Feldstein, "Rethinking International Economic Coordination," Lecture delivered at Nuffield College, Oxford, October 23, 1987, p. 6.

[22] Exchange rate intervention is *sterilized* when the central bank acts to prevent the intervention from affecting the money supply.

an interdependent world, but it is no substitute for responsible domestic economic management.

Because of the difficulties of achieving coordination, some have proposed a return to a Bretton Woods-type target zone system for exchange rates. The rationale for such a system would not be to substitute for coordination but, rather, to apply the discipline of the exchange rate constraint as a means of exerting pressure for coordination.

Tax Burdens and Structure

There are great disparities in both tax burdens and tax structures from nation to nation. Other things being equal, the globalization process enhances the opportunities for tax avoidance and magnifies the competitive advantage of countries with low tax burdens. Of course, other things are often not equal, which can make simplistic tax comparisons misleading. Historically, the total tax burden has been lower in the United States than in most advanced countries, with the notable exception of Japan. But the U.S. revenue structure may put us at a competitive disadvantage because it places a severe burden on capital and discourages saving, largely due to its heavy reliance on income taxes rather than on the consumption taxes emphasized in most other countries. The variety of national tax systems creates complex problems for businesses engaged in international transactions but also provides incentives and opportunities for them to avoid taxes.

Tax Avoidance

Because taxes are an important cost of doing business, businesses find it sometimes pays to relocate in low-tax countries to reduce tax burdens.[23] Global enterprises that have operations in several countries with differing tax burdens may be able to realize their profits in the jurisdictions with the relatively low effective tax rates. Some jurisdictions have attempted to counter such practices by instituting extraterritorial taxation, (i.e., taxing a share of the corporation's total profits, including those earned outside the jurisdiction). Such measures raise controversial jurisdictional questions.

One form of tax avoidance is the creation of tax havens by countries that would not otherwise attract business. Offshore financial centers that accord banks preferential treatment for profits and exempt interest earned by foreigners from taxation are frequently cited examples. Such tax havens are a particularly difficult obstacle to efforts at coordination because unlike most countries, they have little or no incentive to join agreements to harmonize national tax policies.

---

[23] For a discussion of domestic tax policy effects on the international location of direct investment see: Michael J. Boskin, "Tax Policy and the International Location of Investment," in *Taxes and Capital Formation*, ed. Martin Feldstein (Chicago: University of Chicago Press, 1987), pp. 73-80.

Differential tax policies among countries may stimulate healthy competition to lower excessive rates in order to discourage domestic firms from leaving and attract new firms. The practice of countries attracting business by lowering effective tax rates is analogous to the experience of state governments that have reduced taxes in an effort to outbid other states. When carried to extremes, competitive tax reductions could be harmful to participating nations; they can lead to the erosion of the tax base for all involved and little or no net gains in terms of total business activity.[24] This outcome can be avoided by greater cooperation among governments on tax policies.

Competitiveness

The tax structure undoubtedly affects the productivity of domestic industry and, therefore, international competitiveness. Corporate taxes affect competitiveness through the after-tax profitability of capital employed and thus its cost. High after-tax profits are both an incentive for expanding capacity and a means of financing investment. The cost of capital, which includes the cost of the physical assets, interest, depreciation, and taxes, influences the timing, level, and location of investment.[25]

Recent studies of the cost of capital in different countries generally show that the cost of capital has been relatively high in the United States compared with many other advanced countries.[26] Among our competitors, the cost of capital has been very low in Japan, but Germany has a higher cost than the United States. The tax wedge (the difference between the return on capital and the return received by the investor) is generally higher in the United States than in other countries, though West Germany places a greater tax burden on investment. These studies generally apply to years prior to the 1986 Tax Reform Act, which will raise the cost of capital substantially in the United States in future years.

However, credit conditions rather than taxes are the major source of difference in the cost of capital from one country to another. This finding is difficult to reconcile with the view that financial markets are

---

[24] Bryant, *International Financial Intermediation*, pp. 143-144.

[25] The user cost of capital, sometimes called the *rental cost*, can be described as the minimum compensation necessary to make it worthwhile to hold a capital asset when tax aspects and other features of asset ownership are taken into account. See Gary Hufbauer, "The Consumption Tax and International Competitiveness," in *The Consumption Tax*, eds. Charles Walker and Mark Bloomfield (Cambridge, MA: Ballinger Publishing Company, 1987), p. 182.

[26] For a comparison of the cost of capital in the United States, the United Kingdom, West Germany, and Japan, see B. Douglas Bernheim and John Shoven, *Taxation and the Cost of Capital: An International Comparison* (Stanford, CA: Center for Economic Policy Research, Stanford University, August 1986). Calculations in this study were for 1980.

integrated internationally and that they function very well. But empirical studies confirm that large differentials in real interest rates persist and overshadow taxes as a source of variation in capital costs.[27]

It has frequently been proposed that the United States substitute a value-added tax for the corporate income tax as a means of reducing the cost of capital. Studies show that such a change in the tax structure would greatly lower capital costs and improve the international competitiveness of the United States. However, an even larger improvement could be achieved by reducing U.S. interest costs. For this reason, reducing the federal budget deficit and instituting other policies to encourage increased national saving would probably make the greatest contribution to establishing internationally competitive capital costs in the United States.

Another possible effect of taxation on competitiveness relates to GATT rules that permit border adjustments for indirect taxes (heavily relied upon by many other nations) but not for income taxes (heavily relied upon by the United States). Indirect taxes such as general sales taxes can be rebated at the border on exports and imposed at the border on imports. No border tax adjustment is made for corporate income taxes. However, most economists argue that there is no connection between the general tax structure and the U.S. trade balance because excessive border adjustments are completely offset by compensating exchange rate movements.[28]

Historically, tax legislation in the United States has been enacted without much attention to the consequences for the international competitiveness of our industry. High priority should be given to reevaluating tax policy in the global context.

National Saving

Both general macroeconomic policy and the tax structure have a close relationship to the national level of saving. However, the significance of the level of saving for national investment and growth warrants special attention.

Historically, there has been a close association between saving and investment in countries around the world. High-saving countries have tended to be high-investment countries, and low savers low investors. Except in the case of some underdeveloped countries, reliance on foreign capital in recent years has generally been quite limited. But the global integration of financial markets, which permits investors to search worldwide for the highest return commensurate with risk, has encouraged very rapid growth in international capital flows, far exceeding the growth in

---

[27] Time series studies have also shown that credit costs have dominated tax changes as the major source of variation in U.S. capital costs during the past several decades.

[28] This issue is not settled, however. See Hufbauer, "The Consumption Tax and International Competitiveness."

the world economy. In some cases, massive capital flows appear to have broken the link between domestic saving and domestic investment.

If foreign capital can be attracted, it is now quite possible for even a large country to have a high rate of consumption growth without a reduction in its rate of investment, at least for a considerable period of time. The United States is a case in point. In the 1980s, national saving has declined in the United States, but investment has been sustained by massive inflows of foreign capital.

However, relatively little of that investment has been internationally self-financing in the sense of adding enough to this country's ability to earn foreign exchange to cover the cost of servicing the foreign debt incurred. In this circumstance, the U.S. reliance on foreign capital has been very costly. First, it has taken relatively high real interest rates in the United States to attract foreign investment. The resulting high cost of capital has reduced the competitiveness of U.S. producers. Second, because foreigners must acquire dollars to invest in the United States, the demand for dollars increased, and the dollar rose sharply in international currency markets. The higher dollar, in turn, seriously reduced the international competitiveness of domestic producers of tradable goods. This experience indicates that the globalization of markets has not permanently freed low-saving countries from adverse consequences of that behavior so much as it has changed the timing and nature of the hardship incurred.

As the U.S. debt to foreigners grew, the demand for U.S. assets by private foreign investors diminished, and the dollar fell. In some recent periods, attempts by foreign central banks to prevent the dollar from falling farther accounted for all of the net inflows of capital from abroad. If foreign investors should seek to reduce their holdings in the United States, there is a significant risk of a capital crisis, with a depreciating dollar and very high real interest rates severely damaging investment and even inducing a recession. Even if foreign capital inflows continue unabated, the burden of servicing the rising debt to foreigners could significantly handicap the future growth of living standards in the United States.

The globalization of financial markets has increased the range of flexibility of U.S. domestic policy; it reduces the crowding-out effect of domestic budget deficits by permitting temporary international saving inflows to smooth out the path of domestic investment. But the availability of financing from abroad also makes persistent fiscal deficits possible without necessitating sacrifices in current private consumption or investment for years, although not indefinitely. Thus, the international integration of financial markets permits episodes of shortsighted political behavior with respect to the federal budget, up to the point where foreign confidence in dollar assets wanes; after this point is reached, the consequences are very costly for the U.S. economy.

This widened time gap between the short-run benefits and the long-run costs of sustained budget excess is a serious challenge to American economic stability that deserves high-priority study. Although the relatively low level of private saving in the United States is apparently less amenable than government saving (or dissaving) to change by public policies, it also deserves study in this connection.[29]

---

[29] A recent comparative analysis of the relationship of saving, capital formation, and economic growth in the United States and other countries is contained in Robert E. Lipsey and Irving B. Krains, *Saving and Economic Growth: Is the U.S. Really Falling Behind?* (New York: The Conference Board, Inc., 1987).

Chapter 4

MICROECONOMIC EFFECTS OF GLOBALIZATION

The full range of microeconomic policies, from trade policy to business regulation and education policy, is affected by the trend toward international economic integration. However, the nature of the interaction between government intervention in particular sectors of the domestic economy and the globalization of markets is complex. Whereas the effectiveness of many types of domestic business regulation is undermined by world economic integration, the trend toward integration is itself undermined by other types of government intervention that have a distortive effect on international competitiveness.

Trade Policies

One of the principal developments underlying the globalization of markets and production has been the postwar liberalization of international trade. Tariffs have been drastically reduced, and a major push is under way in the Uruguay Round of GATT negotiations to reduce the scope of nontariff barriers such as quotas, voluntary export restraints, and variable import levies.

As the postwar economic leader, the United States identified its own interests with an open and effectively functioning international economic system that brought benefits to all nations. As a result of this policy, and despite the continued existence of many impediments to trade and capital flows, the world is today reaping the benefits of a global economy that is more open and efficient than ever before.

However, as globalization has proceeded, it has become increasingly apparent that some of the most trade-distorting government measures consist of domestic policies applied internally rather than at the border. Notable examples are public subsidies to targeted industries and restrictions on foreign investment that distort international trade in both goods and services. These policies weaken the effectiveness of the conventional forms of border liberalization of trade and capital flows and are therefore incompatible with the globalization of markets.

The persistence of restrictive and distortive practices abroad in the face of the erosion in U.S. economic supremacy has given rise in recent years to calls for a fundamental reorientation of U.S. policy away from our traditional multilateral approach:

U.S. trade policy is at a crossroads: we can either continue to urge other nations to adopt our free-trade economic model or we can change U.S. trade policy to deal with other nations as they are, rather than as we wish they would be. Clearly, only the second course makes sense. It is pure folly for us to presume that we can somehow convince other nations to abandon economic systems that serve their interests and adopt a system that serves ours.[30]

Actually, self-interest is motivating an increasing number of countries in both the East and the West to move toward less interventionist and more market-driven economic systems. In reaction to widespread frustration with government controls, domestic economies are being deregulated, and external transactions are being liberalized. These changes are overwhelmingly a reflection of domestic forces rather than a response to pressures exerted by the United States or any other foreign power.

Furthermore, U.S. trade policy is not predicated on the similarity of other countries' economic systems to our own. Nor has our negotiating strategy been limited to a multilateral approach in which all countries are treated alike. In several GATT codes (e.g., that deal with subsidies), the benefits we offer are extended only to other signatories of the codes, not to all GATT members. The United States has also pursued alternative bilateral approaches, such as the comprehensive free trade agreements negotiated with Israel and Canada.

Recently, however, U.S. bilateralism has been manifest in attempts to open foreign markets under the threat of retaliation if "unfair" foreign restrictions persist. These attempts have been justified by a new and aggressive application of the reciprocity principle in a manner that deviates from the principle's original intent.

Reciprocity

When the Reciprocal Trade Agreement Act was adopted by the United States in 1934, it symbolized a rejection of the intense economic nationalism that had characterized the Great Depression and marked a turning point in attitudes toward international trade. The concept of reciprocity embodied in that act later became the basis for the principle of reciprocity under which seven multilateral rounds of negotiations to liberalize trade were successfully carried out under the aegis of GATT.

As espoused by the United States and applied in GATT, reciprocity meant a broad balance between the reduction in trade barriers offered by the United States and the liberalization obtained collectively from other major trading partners in multilateral negotiations. This concept of reciprocity had three distinguishing features: First, it applied to the negotiations as a whole rather than to individual products, industries, or sectors. Second, it was multilateral rather than bilateral. Third, it was applied in a way that could lead only to reductions of trade barriers, not to increases. To the extent that offers of reductions in barriers could not be broadly matched by other participants, the scope of the liberalization was limited, but the result was not an increase in trade restrictions. With this bias toward opening markets, the principle of reciprocity became a driving force for trade liberalization under American leadership.

---

[30] Pat Choate and Jayne Linger, "Tailored Trade: Dealing," *Harvard Business Review* 66, no. 1 (January-February 1988): pp. 86-93.

In recent years, the United States appears to have implicitly redefined the principle of reciprocity as reflected in both the Administration's actions and the trade bills currently being considered in Congress. Driven by the frustrations over the massive U.S. trade deficits of recent years, both branches of government regard reciprocity as a tool for combating unfair trading practices abroad and establishing a "level playing field."

The new drive for reciprocity departs from all three elements of the original conception. First, it has a strong sectoral theme calling for symmetrical treatment in individual product sectors such as telecommunications equipment and computers. Second, it seeks to force bilateral equivalence in sectoral trading opportunities with individual trading partners even if that entails special liberalizing exceptions applying to no country except the United States. Such exceptions violate the GATT principle of nondiscrimination (the most-favored-nation principle). Third, the new policy is carried out on the basis of threats of retaliation in the form of increases in U.S. trade barriers when this country unilaterally determines that the balance is unfair.

However, trade practices that impede exports and are deemed unfair are not a unique problem faced by U.S. exporters. European Community (EC) exporters, for example, claim that they face similar problems when trading with the United States. In fact, the EC has recently issued an extensive report on significant U.S. trade barriers, including some of questionable consistency with U.S. international obligations.[31] Similarly, developing countries have pointed to U.S. bilateral restraints under the Multifiber Agreement as inconsistent with GATT principles.

Thus, although the threat of denial of access to the huge U.S. market may occasionally serve as an effective negotiating strategy to remedy particularly egregious cases of foreign practices that impede U.S. trade, such actions carry significant dangers. First, it is important to recognize that at the same time U.S. import restrictions harm foreigners, they also impose severe penalties on the U.S. economy. More significant, an aggressive and widespread pursuit of the new reciprocity could lead to a spiral of mutual unraveling of many past gains in opening markets to the detriment of all trading countries.

Given the potential dangers, it is essential that the full implications of restrictive and distortive international trade policies, such as subsidies to targeted industries, be clearly understood. Once the problems are correctly defined, they can be addressed internationally through practical rules and remedies that encourage rather than discourage world trade. From this standpoint, the outcome of the Uruguay Round of GATT negotiations will be crucial.

---

[31] European Community (EC), *1988 Report on U.S. Trade Barriers* (Brussels: EC, December 1987).

Domestic Subsidies

Although export subsidies on nonprimary products are prohibited under GATT, domestic subsidies are not. Indeed, they are recognized in the subsidies code as legitimate instruments of national economic and social policy. Because domestic subsidies do not distinguish between goods sold at home and abroad, the presumption is that their main purpose is to further some generally accepted national objective rather than to provide an artificial advantage in foreign trade. Nevertheless, domestic subsidies are open to challenge and to possible countermeasures by importing countries on the grounds of material injury to the importer's domestic industry.

The problem is the uncertainty about the types of domestic incentives that should be subject to countervailing action. One possibility would be to make a list of potentially troublesome subsidies comparable to the illustrative list of export subsidies in the present code. Another would be to identify categories of subsidies that would be acceptable and therefore exempt from countervailing measures (e.g., subsidies designed to further adjustment by downsizing or phasing out particular noncompetitive industries or across-the-board subsidies not targeted to specific industries).

Industrial policy in support of specific industries has become a major source of international trade friction, especially when the targeting is directed at technology-intensive industries such as semiconductors (Japan) or aircraft (the European Airbus). Yet, a case can be made for government support for some basic research and development activities in high-technology fields on the grounds of the external economies they generate. Because the benefits of investment in such activities cannot be fully appropriated by the investing firms but are reaped in part by other firms, the volume of private investment in technology-intensive industries may be below the social optimum. The argument has been made, therefore, that government subsidization of research and development should not be subject to countervailing action, especially when the knowledge generated becomes available not only to domestic firms but to foreign firms as well. However, the line between legitimate support for research and development and questionable subsidization of the commercial application of new discoveries is often unclear.

Unrestrained subsidization of targeted industries results in contrived comparative advantage and therefore runs counter to the rational globalization of markets. A more precise international consensus is needed on the difficult problem of domestic subsidies, particularly as they apply to research and development in technology-intensive industries.

The subsidization of agricultural exports has been a subject of bitter dispute, especially between the United States and the EC. However, these export subsidies are basically driven by domestic agricultural-support programs that generate huge surpluses. Only by addressing the domestic policies that are the root cause of the problem can the issue of agricultural export subsidies be effectively resolved. The United States has introduced a proposal along these lines in the Uruguay Round.

Trade-Related Foreign Investment Restrictions

Two types of restrictions on foreign investment directly distort international trade: trade-related performance requirements and restrictions that inhibit international transactions in services which require physical proximity between the provider and the user.

Performance Requirements. These are conditions placed on the operation of foreign enterprise by host governments in the form of minimum export levels or local-content requirements. By pressuring firms toward economic behavior inconsistent with market forces, they distort trade and investment flows, lead to uneconomic use of resources, and harm the interests of other countries.

Minimum export requirements are similar in effect to export subsidies: They artificially increase exports above levels that would have prevailed in the absence of the intervention. The exports may displace another country's home production or its sales to third markets. Producers can usually recoup losses on such uneconomic exports by exploiting protected positions in the host-country market. Local-content requirements artificially reduce imports by mandating that a given percentage of the value of the final product be produced locally or pur-chased from local sources. Often, the two types of requirements are combined by linking a firm's permitted imports to the value of its exports so that no net direct foreign exchange costs result from its operations.

Performance requirements are enforced through a variety of incentives and disincentives. Foreign enterprises that do not comply may be barred from a host country or subject to various penalties. Conversely, incentives such as tax concessions and import protection may be offered to firms willing to adhere to performance requirements.

Trade-distorting investment measures should be made subject to international discipline so that those demonstrably damaging to other countries' interests are avoided or eliminated. At the initiative of the United States, these practices have been included on the agenda of the current GATT negotiations; but thus far, not much progress has been made in reaching an agreement.

Service Transactions. In most developed countries, services constitute a major share of the economy, accounting for 40 to 50 percent of nongovernment GNP and a substantially larger percentage of employment. Moreover, most new-job creation has been concentrated in the service sector.

International trade in services has expanded rapidly and now equals about $500 billion, or one-quarter of the volume of trade in goods. As in other aspects of the globalization of markets, advances in telecommunications have enormously facilitated the operation of service industries on a worldwide scale.

The central problem in service trade is the complex of restrictions that inhibit realization of the potential advantages of international specialization. Although some of the restrictions are the conventional border measures such as tariffs and import quotas, the most important distortions are investment-related. They affect services such as banking, insurance, and advertising, where, as a practical matter, physical proximity between provider and user is necessary or highly advantageous. In effect, therefore, trade liberalization in many service sectors implies the freedom of domestic firms to establish affiliates abroad and to be accorded national treatment (i.e., treatment equal to that granted to firms of host-country nationality).

At present, service firms attempting to operate abroad are frequently confronted with limitations on the right of establishment, discriminatory taxes or regulations, restrictions on access to local distribution facilities (including transportation and communication networks), and other deviations from national treatment. As in the case of trade-related performance requirements, the United States has taken the lead in pushing for liberalization in this field. Recently, it introduced a proposal for a framework agreement on trade in services at the Uruguay Round. The adverse effects of trade-related investment measures are sufficiently urgent to warrant further study to expose their negative consequences and point to appropriate corrective policies.

The Regulation of Business

Government regulation of business extends to most industries in the United States and typically to many stages of a firm's operations. Globalization can be either a blessing or a curse insofar as government intervention is concerned, cutting through and pressuring against excessive regulation on the one hand and undermining needed regulation on the other.

The international integration of markets complicates and reduces the effectiveness of many types of business regulation. But not all domestic regulations are significantly affected. In contrast to the regulation of the production process itself, many types of domestic product regulation, for example, appear to be largely unaffected. Generally, each country can enforce its own national standards for products regardless of the origin of the product. In some instances, however, domestic standards may place domestic producers at a disadvantage in world markets and foreign producers at a disadvantage in domestic markets.

The more highly integrated the markets are, the more likely that regulatory problems have already been encountered and investigated. For example, the effects of globalization on the regulation of financial institutions have been studied quite extensively in recent years, and there have already been some attempts at greater harmonization. But the impact in many other areas, such as environmental and antitrust regulations, has not yet received much attention. Many experts in the regulatory field are coming to recognize the influence of global markets, however, and agree on the need to investigate the potential benefits and costs of harmonizing regulatory standards across countries.

Financial Regulation.

There is a long history of national regulation of domestic financial institutions in the United States and most other developed countries. Regulations were often created to serve a prudential function: to ensure the stability of the whole system (lender of last resort) or to protect individual depositors and investors. Monetary policy is also a form of national control of financial institutions, though its purpose is generally to influence real activity and prices. In addition, financial institutions, like other businesses, are subject to regulations intended to limit the concentration of power and ensure competition. (State governments are often quite active in this field.)

The globalization of financial markets has proceeded at an exceptional rate in the past decade, outpacing international integration in other economic sectors. Changing technology has encouraged new types of financial intermediation, frequently across national borders. The rise in cross-border transactions permits greater diversification of risk and increased opportunities for the financing of business activity. Recent experience suggests, however, that international integration may also increase the potential for financial market instability. And regulators of financial institutions must adjust continually to new financial instruments and other innovations, which are frequently developed in response to regulation itself.

Because the regulation of financial institutions differs in critical ways from one nation to another, competitive inequities develop that provide strong incentives for financial institutions to locate their activities in countries with less stringent regulations.[32] With financial markets so highly integrated, financial institutions have a great deal of latitude in locating operations. For this reason, competition among nations to attract financial businesses makes it very difficult for regulatory authorities to maintain national preferences in regulation, even when they are thought to be necessary to prevent unsound practices.[33] Even financial business that is fundamentally domestic is often conducted through international transactions to enable the participants to avoid domestic regulations.

The international integration of financial markets greatly complicates oversight of financial institutions. For example, domestic regulators in some countries may not be able to prevent banks from transferring bad or imprudent loans to the balance sheets of offices abroad. The on-site bank supervisors may not have sufficient information to evaluate a loan made abroad. As a result, a multinational bank could play one nation's supervisory authorities off against others. A similar problem arises from

[32] Different tax treatments also provide strong location incentives. See "Tax Burdens and Structure," p. 25.

[33] Bryant, *International Financial Intermediation*, Chapter 7.

differential regulations pertaining to the capital adequacy of banks. Because these regulations have influenced bank location decisions, serious questions about both soundness and efficiency have arisen.[34]

The global operations of financial institutions also raise serious jurisdictional questions for regulators responsible for overseeing the stability of the financial system. For example, should a central bank have responsibility for providing the lender-of-last-resort function for the foreign operations of domestically owned banks and/or for the domestic operations of foreign-owned banks?

In the securities industry, jurisdictional disputes have arisen concerning disclosure requirements. Some nations' regulators have not always cooperated when other governments attempt to extend their reach to cover escaping parties. Attempts by the United States to enforce Securities and Exchange Commission (SEC) disclosure requirements and commodity futures regulations extraterritorially have been met with serious objections from foreign leaders.[35]

Opinions differ on how to deal with regulatory issues arising from the globalization of financial markets. One view is that the pressure for deregulation should be encouraged because it helps to cut through excessive regulatory interference and impels modernization of antiquated regulation. At the other extreme is the view that the prudential risks are so high that barriers to international integration should be erected to help restore the effectiveness of regulation or at least prevent any further competitive deregulation.

A third approach could be to delegate authority over regulation to an international body such as the IMF. The advantage of this method would be that regulation could be retained without losing the benefits arising from the integration of markets. The disadvantage would be that nations would lose their autonomy in the area of financial regulation.

Finally, cooperative efforts by the regulatory bodies of different nations might achieve a sufficient degree of harmonization to encourage prudent practices and prevent inefficient location decisions. Progress has already been made with negotiations concerning capital requirements for banks.

Whatever approach to reconciling divergent national financial policies is chosen, it would be greatly enhanced by early agreement by both government officials and market participants on the desirable scope of financial regulation. Such a consensus would improve the chances for success of any further efforts at international harmonization.

---

[34] Bryant, *International Financial Intermediation*, p. 142.

[35] Richard Cooper and Ann L. Hollick, "International Relations in a Technologically Advanced Future" in *International Frontiers and Foreign Relations*, ed. Anne Keatly (Washington, D.C.: National Academy Press, 1985), p. 252.

Intellectual Property Rights

Intellectual property rights are another area of domestic regulation that has been greatly affected by globalization. Intellectual property is a fundamental business asset that is protected in the United States by patents, copyrights, and trademarks. This protection is a powerful incentive for business innovation and creativity. But the disparity in regulation and enforcement from country to country has made it more difficult to earn an adequate return on innovative products and services as markets become increasingly integrated.

Many corporations have suffered severe losses because of inadequate protection of intellectual property rights in some countries. With the rapid expansion of international trade involving intellectual property, the losses due to inadequate protection have grown huge. One estimate puts losses due to counterfeiting at $6 to $8 billion a year. Particularly heavy losses have been reported by the U.S. computer software, pharmaceutical, electronics, and agricultural chemicals industries.[36]

Some countries have tightened regulations or are planning to do so. But many still have only minimal protection. International agreements on intellectual property rights are generally lacking in effective enforcement procedures. U.S. aid to affected companies usually takes the form of import controls on goods with counterfeit trademarks and time-consuming bilateral negotiations to upgrade standards in countries where protection is lagging.

This is an area where harmonization and administration of policies at a supernational level might be more efficient and, in the long run, beneficial to all countries. The United States is pressing for a comprehensive agreement in the present round of GATT negotiations. If efforts in GATT are not successful, high priority should be given to the study of other approaches to achieving adequate standards and effective enforcement of intellectual property rights.

U.S. Antitrust Law

U.S. antitrust law also fails to reflect the realities of changing global competition. Although foreign competition is often taken into account in enforcement, the laws themselves are focused on domestic market conditions. The globalization of markets and increasing international competition necessitate a new look at the underlying principles of these antiquated laws.[37]

---

[36] Kenneth W. Dam, "The Growing Importance of International Protection of Intellectual Property," *The International Lawyer* 12, no. 3 (Summer 1987): pp. 627-638.

[37] President's Commission on Industrial Competitiveness, *Global Competition: The New Reality*, vol. 2 (Washington, D.C.: U.S. Government Printing Office, 1985).

The broad U.S. commitment to an economy based on competition is reflected in antitrust policies that extend back to the Sherman Antitrust Act of 1890, the Clayton Act of 1914, and the Federal Trade Commission Act of 1914. Basically, these laws prohibit artificial restraints on the operation of market forces, prevent individual business firms from dominating markets, and prohibit price discrimination.

When the major antitrust laws were enacted, and when amendments were passed in the early postwar years, U.S. business firms did not face the intense competition from foreign producers that they must contend with today. U.S. companies were often dominant in world markets and were not threatened by foreign competition. In today's increasingly global markets, however, the whole context of competition has changed, and it can no longer be defined in terms of domestic firms.

U.S. companies conduct thousands of international transactions that raise possible antitrust issues, including overseas distribution agreements, joint ventures, joint research and development agreements, mergers with foreign firms, and agreements on patents, trademarks, and technology transfers. In many cases, although the transactions do not involve conflict with antitrust laws, concern about their potential application can inhibit business operations and cause firms to abandon or limit innovative international activities.

Ambiguity and uncertainty created by the application of antitrust law are a major issue. The laws do not provide specific guidance for business decisions; rather, they set forth broad principles of general application. Certain types of business activities, such as price-fixing and territorial allocation of markets, are regarded as illegal under the antitrust laws, but companies often have difficulty determining whether a specific transaction represents a violation. Moreover, many believe that the history of antitrust legislation has not provided sufficient guidance to either the enforcement agencies or the courts.

American companies are at a disadvantage when foreign competitors are not hampered by the types of restrictions imposed by U.S. antitrust laws. Although most of our trading partners have their own antitrust laws, they often permit activities regarded as illegal under U.S. laws. The ambiguities in the definition of competition in the United States' laws as well as the leeway existing in the antitrust laws of major U.S. foreign competitors suggest that our antitrust policy needs to be reexamined in a global context.

U.S. companies are also handicapped as exporters and international investors by the extraterritorial application of U.S. antitrust laws. Firms must make sure that their foreign operations do not violate domestic antitrust laws while at the same time being subject to the laws of the foreign country.

32

In order to enhance the vigor of American business while preserving a competitive environment, the Administration recently has proposed comprehensive reform of U.S. antitrust laws.[38] The proposals include the following:

- Amend Section 7 of the Clayton Act to distinguish more clearly between procompetitive mergers and mergers that would create a significant probability of increased prices to consumers.

- Limit private and government antitrust actions to actual (rather than triple) damages except for damages caused by overcharges or underpayments.

- Remove unwarranted and cumbersome restrictions on interlocking directorates.

- Clarify the application of U.S. antitrust laws in cases involving international trade where the plaintiff is a U.S. private company.

- Require that any antitrust claims remaining against other defendants after a partial settlement in a case be appropriately reduced.

Efforts are also being made by the Organization for Economic Cooperation and Development to foster greater cooperation in antitrust enforcement among member countries. The success of these efforts could contribute to reducing the ambiguities and jurisdictional conflicts involved in U.S. antitrust laws.

A revision in U.S. antitrust laws to formally recognize the increased integration of markets and the strength of foreign competitors seems appropriate. But increased foreign competition does not eliminate the possibility that international cartels will develop, severely reducing worldwide competition. International coordination of antitrust policy may be necessary to discourage such developments.

Experts in the antitrust field do not agree about the need for reforming antitrust legislation. Some believe that the current legislation is satisfactory as long as the regulators take the globalization of markets into account in their enforcement practices. Others feel that the uncertainty created by existing legislation needs to be dealt with promptly.

Although reform of U.S. antitrust laws seems appropriate, it does not appear to deserve as high a priority as several other areas of reform discussed in this document.

---

[38] Message of President Ronald Reagan to the 99th Congress, February 19, 1987.

Environmental Regulation

Since the creation of the Environmental Protection Agency in 1970, a number of bills aimed at restoring American land, air, and water quality have been passed. This area of regulation has been widely criticized as compromising the economy's efficiency and reducing the international competitiveness of U.S. industry.

A recent cross-country study by the Congressional Budget Office[39] found that output and productivity losses attributable to environmental regulation were relatively greater in the United States than in Canada, West Germany, and Japan. Expenditures on pollution control as a percentage of gross domestic product were significantly higher in the United States than in the other three countries, and it is likely that even greater discrepancies in terms of expenditures and standards exist between the United States and less developed countries. Nevertheless, except for a limited number of industries (e.g., the U.S. nonferrous metals industry), the effect of environmental standards on U.S. international competitiveness appears to be minor.

In the United States, the benefits from environmental regulations in terms of a safer and healthier quality of life are widely recognized. However, some less developed countries have chosen to become pollution havens, thereby sacrificing their environment for economic reasons. They could be seen as exporting environmental quality to the United States along with their lower-priced goods. At some point, however, these countries too will need to raise their environmental standards and expenditures to be more consistent with those of developed countries, both for their own sake and for the world's.

One can ask whether pollution control should be a necessary aspect of modern production for all nations. Condemnation of polluters seems particularly appropriate for types of pollution that damage the environment beyond the borders of the offending nation and where the benefit of pollution reduction would be correspondingly dispersed.

Pollution controls affect production costs. The question arises, therefore, whether the concept of unfair trade practices should include the failure of a country to maintain environmental standards or the subsidization by a government of private-sector pollution-abatement costs. If so, should the equivalent of antidumping or countervailing duties be imposed on imports from such a country?

This issue was addressed by the OECD in 1972 when it adopted a set of principles to guide the industrial countries in their trade policy regarding environmental measures. In essence, the principles recognize the legitimacy of differences in national environmental standards that reflect such factors as differences in income levels and the assimilative capacity of the environment. A country's exports should therefore not be penalized

---

[39] Congressional Budget Office, *Environmental Regulation and Economic Efficiency* (Washington, D.C.: U.S. Government Printing Office, March 1985).

through trade restrictions for its failure to maintain the same environmental standards as other countries. When pollution-abatement costs are incurred in the private sector, however, they should be borne there rather than by the government so that market prices will more accurately reflect the social costs of production. To the extent that this "polluter-pays" principle is followed, border tax adjustments to offset differences in environmental costs are unjustified.

These principles have served as guidelines for the industrial countries, but many developing countries have not subscribed to them. Nor have the nations of the Third World developed any guidelines of their own. With the rapid growth of developing country trade in an integrated global economy, Third World nations should be encouraged to develop a set of guidelines in the environmental field that minimize distortions in international trade.

Labor Regulation

Discrepancies among various countries' labor practices take on greater significance for domestic industries as markets become more integrated. The suppression of workers' rights does not appear to be widespread, but where such practices exist, they may enhance the competitiveness of domestic firms, at least in the short run. However, it must be recognized that labor standards vary widely and that in some European countries such standards exceed those in the United States.

One of the provisions of the Omnibus Trade Bill recently vetoed by the President addressed the question of labor standards. Included in the bill's definition of an unreasonable trade practice mandating retaliation was a "persistent pattern of conduct" that denies to workers the right of association and the right to organize and bargain collectively, permits forced or compulsory labor, fails to provide a minimum age for employment, and fails to provide standards for minimum wages, hours, and occupational safety and health.

In addition to the need to demonstrate a persistent pattern rather than isolated incidents of violations of labor standards, action under this provision of the bill was subject to two further exceptions. The United States would not retaliate if the foreign country is demonstrating significant improvement in standards or if the practices are not inconsistent with the country's level of economic development.

At the time this paper was going to press, Congress was considering a revised trade bill that would meet the President's objections to the original bill. The revised bill is likely to include the same provisions for international labor standards as the original bill. Assuming that the wide-ranging qualifications in the original bill are retained, the danger that the workers' rights provision will be used as a cover for protectionist actions is substantially reduced. At the same time, the possibility exists that the provision may induce an improvement in labor standards abroad, particularly in some newly industrialized countries where they may be lagging.

Export Controls

In today's market environment, where increasing globalization of production and diffusion of technology are taking place, U.S. export controls often appear to be outmoded, unnecessarily reducing the ability of American firms to compete abroad.[40]

U.S. export control regulations are the result of legislation aimed at important national security and foreign policy goals. Unfortunately, the controls have often put U.S. exporters at a competitive disadvantage without effectively preventing diversion of high-technology goods to potential adversaries. Moreover, these regulations have damaged the reputations of U.S. producers as reliable suppliers, and potential customers have been forced to rely on competing foreign suppliers. Increasingly, U.S. exporters have found that competing producers in Europe and Japan have picked up their lost export business.

Although U.S. export controls are imposed in cooperation with our allies through the Coordinating Committee on Multilateral Export Controls (COCOM), they tend to be tighter and wider in scope than those applied by other COCOM countries. When controls are not applied uniformly among the member countries and the same products are readily available from foreign sources, the effectiveness of U.S. controls is severely undermined, and American business firms lose sales to foreign competitors. Without multilateral cooperation and unity of purpose, U.S. export control policy cannot achieve its stated objectives; it only serves to transfer export opportunities to our competitors.

Government attempts to enforce export controls on the foreign subsidiaries of U.S. firms and to prevent the reexport of U.S. technology by foreign companies have created serious jurisdictional disputes between the United States and other countries. In some cases, business firms have been faced with conflicting regulations from different national governments.

A recent study by the National Academy of Sciences[41] summarized the major problems with U.S. export controls.

- The scope of current U.S. export controls encompasses too many products and technologies to be administered effectively. In particular, the U.S. government has not provided a justification for the continued control of low-level

---

[40] President's Commission on Industrial Competitiveness, *Global Competition: The New Reality*, vols. 1 and 2 (Washington, D.C.: U.S. Government Printing Office, 1985); National Academy of Sciences, *Balancing the National Interest: National Security Export Controls and Global Economic Competition* (Washington, D.C.: National Academy Press, 1987); and Committee for Economic Development, *Toll of the Twin Deficits* (New York: 1987).

[41] National Academy of Sciences, *Balancing the National Interest: National Security Export Controls and Global Economic Competition*.

technologies--such as those technologies which are found to be of marginal military significance or which are available from foreign sources with little or no restrictions.

- Delays in the licensing process or uncertainty about obtaining an applicable export license often result in lost export sales.

- U.S. producers, especially small-to-medium-sized firms, are deterred from exporting by the complexities and delays of the export control regulations.

- Foreign customers are discouraged from relying on U.S. suppliers because of uncertainties about future license approvals, follow-on service, availability of parts and components, and possible reexport constraints.

- From a global perspective, some aspects of the U.S. export controls (particularly reexport controls) are also seen as conflicting with widely accepted principles of international law and national sovereignty. The extraterritorial aspects of U.S. export controls tend to create mistrust among U.S. allies as well as resentment against U.S. policy. As a consequence, the legal justifications of U.S. export controls have been weakened, and foreign compliance with U.S. restrictions has become less than satisfactory.

U.S. export control policy requires a delicate balancing of national security needs and foreign policy objectives on the one hand and export competitiveness of U.S. firms on the other. In response to the urging of the U.S. business community, the Administration recently undertook a series of regulatory reforms and reorganized the export control agency.[42] The regulatory modifications are designed to reduce administrative burdens on exporters, strengthen enforcement of export laws, and enhance America's export competitiveness. The Administration also established a new Bureau of Export Administration within the Department of Commerce as a central agency charged with: (a) developing export control policy, (b) processing license applications, (c) developing foreign availability studies to determine when products should be decontrolled, and (d) enforcing U.S. export control laws. These changes are intended to minimize the negative impact of the U.S. export control policy on U.S. international competitiveness and to help U.S. exporters better adapt to the increasingly global environment. While these unilateral reforms represent significant improvement, much more needs to be done in achieving coordination among all COCOM countries in the management of export control policy. A multilateral approach to export controls is increasingly important in today's global environment.

---

[42] U.S. Department of Commerce, *Business America* 109, no. 5 (February 19, 1988).

Chapter 5

THE CHANGED U.S. ROLE IN THE WORLD

Between 1950 and 1982, the U.S. share of the GNP of the world's market economies fell from almost one-half to less than one-third. In the 1950s, the relative decline largely reflected the rapid recovery of Europe from World War II, a development welcomed by the United States and assisted in a variety of ways, most notably by the Marshall Plan. The subsequent decline stemmed partly from a continuing lag in productivity growth behind Europe but mainly from the spectacular growth of Japan and other Asian countries. In longer-term perspective, the lag behind other countries may be partly a reflection of the historical phenomenon of convergence, causing nations that were previously behind in their level of productivity to grow faster than the leader.[43]

During the same postwar period, U.S. exports also dropped as a share of the total exports of market economies from about 18 percent to less than 13 percent. The main counterpart of this decline was the precipitous rise in the shares of Japan--from 1.4 percent to 8.4 percent-- and the newly industrialized countries of Asia.

More worrisome than the lag of U.S. economic performance behind that of Japan, Germany, and a number of other countries is the retardation in the growth of U.S. productivity below its own historical trend. Not only has U.S. productivity growth since 1973 fallen short of the rapid rate achieved over the previous quarter century, but it has also lagged behind the longer-term U.S. trend of the pre-World War II period. The retardation in productivity growth adversely affects both our standard of living and our competitiveness in world markets.

Implications for U.S. Leadership

The lag in U.S. economic progress has not by itself undermined the U.S. position as world economic leader. After all, the United States still weighs more heavily than any other single country on the world economic scales. Moreover, the reconstruction of Europe and Japan and the narrowing of the gap between rich and poor nations have been cornerstones of American foreign economic policy since the Second World War.

What threatens to erode U.S. influence, however, is the perception that we are incapable of managing our economic affairs responsibly and living within our means. With an annual current-account deficit of about

---

[43] William J. Baumol, "Productivity Growth, Convergence, and Welfare: What the Long-Run Data Show," *American Economic Review* 76, no. 6 (December 1986): pp. 1072-1085.

$140 billion, more than 3 percent of our spending on goods and services is being financed by the savings of foreigners.

World leadership is made up of many elements. One of the key requirements is to be the world's lender of last resort, as demonstrated by the United States in the Marshall Plan. When Europe was in ruins after the Second World War and Communist takeovers in France and Italy seemed possible, the United States came to the rescue. Between 1948 and 1951, we provided $12.5 billion in grant assistance (equivalent to more than $100 billion in today's dollars). Currently, our rising net debt to foreigners is a major inhibitor of our exercise of world leadership.

Unless the United States is in a position to take bold initiatives and, if necessary, to commit real resources to the solution of critical world problems, it cannot lead. Because of the budget deficit, the U.S. bilateral foreign aid budget has been cut, and we have become a drag on others' initiatives to step up multilateral assistance. The Baker Plan addresses the Third World debt crisis, but its impact has been far less than it could be because insofar as U.S. government resources are concerned, the plan is an empty box. Today, we are a profligate borrower internationally rather than the lender of last resort.

The danger in the current situation is that no other country is likely to assume the mantle of leadership in the world political economy. Even if Japan were willing to bear the cost, it is habituated to a low-profile role in the world; and in any event, few countries are as yet ready to follow Japanese leadership. As for the EC, no single country is of adequate economic size; and collectively, European decision making requires the agreement of twelve sovereign countries--hardly a prescription for quick action in a crisis.

Security

The implications of declining U.S. economic supremacy extend well beyond issues of international trade and finance. Our security arrangements in Europe and the Pacific were basically established in the early postwar period, when neither Western Europe nor Japan had fully recovered from the war and when their per capita incomes and technical and industrial capacities were far below our own. It was natural at that time for the United States to assume the main burden of defense against the common danger of Soviet aggression in Europe and Asia.

Today, despite its huge and unsustainable budgetary and external payments deficits, the United States still bears a disproportionate share of the defense burden (see Table 2, p. 39). American military expenditures are larger than those of all other members of the North Atlantic Treaty Organization and Japan put together, amounting currently to two-thirds of the cost of the common defense. As a percentage of gross domestic product, our expenditures far exceed those of our allies, and each American spends more than twice as much as any citizen of an allied country to finance what is essentially a collective responsibility.

TABLE 2

DEFENSE SPENDING

	Spending (billions)	As % of Gross Domestic Product	Spending Per Person
United States	$281.10	6.8%	$1,164
France	28.46	3.9	516
West Germany	27.69	3.1	454
Britain	27.33	5.1	481
Japan	19.84	1.0	163
Italy	13.46	2.2	235
Canada	7.90	2.2	308

Source: Department of Defense as reproduced in The New York Times, May 20, 1988, p. A14.

Now that per capita incomes and technical progress in the industrial nations have converged, some realignment of the burden of defense costs appears warranted. But how and to what extent depend on the role the United States wants to play in the world.

No other country in the non-Communist world has emerged to replace the United States as the leader in either the economic or the defense realm. However, if this country is to sustain its leadership in the absence of economic supremacy, it must change its approach to take into account the increased economic strength of other industrial nations and the rising economic importance and political influence of many countries in the Third World.

Effective leadership in this kind of world demands a greater proportion of consensus building and mutual cooperation relative to unilateral action. In addition, a world leader must set an example at home in the management of its economic and social affairs. And it must have a realistic vision of its own development and that of the world and the resources, desire, and ability to pursue that vision.

National Industrial Base

As a general rule, the United States does not have an explicit national industrial base policy. Recently, however, the Department of Defense and others have expressed concern about the impact of globalization on the U.S. industrial base.[44] The spread of technology worldwide, the mobility of capital, other nations' industrial policies, and other global factors prevent the United States or any single country from being a leader in all fields of production and technology. Over time, a succession of products has begun to disappear from commercial production in the United States, and this country has lost its technological lead in a number of areas.

The Defense Department has identified numerous declining industries as crucial to national security. Machine tools, optics, semiconductors, and steel are among the militarily significant industries adversely affected by global market forces, and the Defense Department has expressed great concern about these and other sectors. The department fears that the United States is losing its ability not only to produce technically advanced products but also to develop new technologies.

Although the United States is not the industrial leader it was in the 1950s, it is not in a state of industrial deterioration either. U.S. industries that take advantage of the globalization process by sourcing and moving internationally will flourish, balancing those industries that decline. However, from a military viewpoint, the issue is the composition of the domestic industrial base.

The importance of the military industrial base should be recognized, and steps should be taken to ensure that it does not decline to a dangerous level. Realistic and well-documented policy recommendations to achieve this goal deserve high priority. At the same time, policy makers should be on guard against the use of national security arguments as a cloak for protectionism.

Among the plausible proposals for improving the U.S. industrial base are policies that increase emphasis on scientific and technological education, stimulate greater research and development efforts by both the public and the private sectors, and encourage the overall adaptation of U.S. industries to global factors. For those U.S. industries critical to the national security, the Defense Department's strategy should be one of cooperation--with our industries, with our allies, and with our allies' industries. If economic circumstances make domestic sourcing impossible, secure systems of foreign-site sourcing will need to be worked out.

---

[44] The views expressed in this section have benefited from recent discussions between CED and the Defense Department.

Education

Modern societies have long recognized the important contribution to economic growth made by educating and training the labor force. Obviously, advanced training is central to the maintenance of a lead in science and technology. Modern production techniques also require a labor force that is well trained in basic skills and able to adapt quickly to successive new technologies. In short, education is an investment in human capital and is as essential to productivity growth as investment in physical capital.

In a global economy characterized by the rapid transfer of technology and resources, the economic benefits of education quickly diffuse across national borders. In a highly competitive world, the result of this transfer is improved availability of low-cost, high-quality products. Society gains not only from improved products but also from the increased mobility of an educated labor force. The United States has benefited greatly from the immigration of highly trained foreigners, and foreign countries have benefited from the training their citizens have received in U.S. institutions of higher education.

At the other extreme, the relatively large portion of the U.S. population that is poorly trained is a heavy burden for the nation to carry. The forgone output is a costly loss, and the special welfare assistance and crime-related programs are a social burden.

In a highly integrated global economy, a nation that falls behind in the education and training of its labor force will not remain a leading economic power. If the United States is to remain competitive while achieving satisfactory economic progress for its people, the reality of global integration requires that improvements in our education and training programs be given high priority in both government and private planning. Among these improvements should be curricular changes at all levels designed to convey an understanding of the global economy.

Chapter 6

<u>POLICY STRATEGIES</u>

As the forces of globalization become more pervasive in our economic life, domestic economic policies will adjust to the new circumstances in various ways. We have already observed both counterproductive responses, such as the rise in protectionist sentiment, and positive responses, such as the recent international agreement to harmonize capital requirements in banking. How policy makers here and abroad respond to globalization will significantly influence the contribution this process will make to our economic well-being.

One strategy is a do-nothing policy. In some areas, particularly in financial regulation, this can result in de facto deregulation, a situation in which domestic regulations become ineffective. Not surprisingly, some view the globalization process as an opportunity to hasten deregulation. On the other hand, a no-change policy that attempts to enforce the existing regulations with no recognition of the changing international economic situation can result in the relocation of business firms to other countries, a process that can be costly for the domestic economy in terms of jobs, output, and the tax base.

At the other extreme, policy makers may respond to the international integration of markets by erecting barriers to globalization. The barriers may be intended to reduce competition or to help regulators preserve domestic priorities. The danger in a strategy of raising barriers to trade in goods and services is that it invites retaliation and reduces economic growth. However, some believe that certain types of international capital movements should be discouraged because there is evidence that speculation can result in damaging variability in exchange rates. But we believe that restrictions on capital flows would be very damaging.[45]

A more constructive strategy than either the do-nothing approach or the building of barriers entails some form of cooperation among nations to promote the achievement of mutually desired goals. Cooperative strategies involve a continuum ranging from some form of world government at one extreme to the mere exchange of information at the other. Because nations desire autonomy, there is little sentiment favoring international government except for very limited purposes. As a practical matter, negotiated cooperation is the most that can be achieved in most cases, and

---

[45] Some years ago, James Tobin proposed an internationally uniform transfer tax on transactions across currencies. The purpose of such a tax would be to increase the transaction costs of short-run purchases and sales of assets made for speculative purposes. Such barriers could be imposed unilaterally or in cooperation with other nations. The disadvantages of the proposal are summarized in Bryant, *International Financial Intermediation*, pp. 153-157.

there is no guarantee that its result will be optimal. Until recently, negotiations have successfully reduced barriers to trade. Some limited success has also been achieved in international agreements to coordinate macroeconomic policies, and it now appears that progress is being made in negotiations to harmonize some aspects of banking regulation. But in most areas of regulation, there has been little or no attempt to negotiate differences.

Nationalistic politics, differing national goals, and other considerations may impose a practical limit on opportunities for negotiating international agreements on economic policy. But the United States can benefit by making some accommodations to globalization on its own. In enacting new legislation or administering existing regulations, greater weight should be given to the international consequences of these actions and their impact on U.S. competitiveness. Too often in the past, U.S. policy makers have neglected these considerations, and a continuation of that habit will prove increasingly detrimental to the U.S. economy.

To improve national understanding of the forces of globalization and to ensure that those forces are taken into account in public policy formation, further study of the issues raised in this paper is needed. Such studies will help to clarify changes required in existing policies and regulations. They will also suggest strategic approaches for future policy making that will enable the nation to reap the benefits of an increasingly integrated world economy while minimizing the costs.

Committee for Economic Development
477 Madison Avenue
New York, New York 10022